Francis Frith's
HERTFORDSHIRE

◆

PHOTOGRAPHIC MEMORIES

Francis Frith's

HERTFORDSHIRE

◆

Keith Howell

First published in the United Kingdom in 2000 by
Frith Book Company Ltd

Paperback Edition 2000
ISBN 1-85937-247-3

Hardback Reprinted in 2000
ISBN 1-85937-079-9

British Library Cataloguing in Publication Data

Francis Frith's Hertfordshire
Keith Howell

Frith Book Company Ltd
Frith's Barn, Teffont,
Salisbury, Wiltshire SP3 5QP
Tel: +44 (0) 1722 716 376
Email: info@frithbook.co.uk
www.frithbook.co.uk

Printed and bound in Great Britain

The Author would like to thank the staff at Hertfordshire Archives and Local Studies
for their kind assistance.

CONTENTS

FRANCIS FRITH: *Victorian Pioneer*

FRANCIS FRITH, Victorian founder of the world-famous photographic archive, was a complex and multitudinous man. A devout Quaker and a highly successful Victorian businessman, he was both philosophic by nature and pioneering in outlook.

By 1855 Francis Frith had already established a wholesale grocery business in Liverpool, and sold it for the astonishing sum of £200,000, which is the equivalent today of over £15,000,000. Now a multi-millionaire, he was able to indulge his passion for travel. As a child he had pored over travel books written by early explorers, and his fancy and imagination had been stirred by family holidays to the sublime mountain regions of Wales and Scotland. 'What a land of spirit-stirring and enriching scenes and places!' he had written. He was to return to these scenes of grandeur in later years to 'recapture the thousands of vivid and tender memories', but with a different purpose. Now in his thirties, and captivated by the new science of photography, Frith set out on a series of pioneering journeys to the Nile regions that occupied him from 1856 until 1860.

INTRIGUE AND ADVENTURE

He took with him on his travels a specially-designed wicker carriage that acted as both dark-room and sleeping chamber. These far-flung journeys were packed with intrigue and adventure. In his life story, written when he was sixty-three, Frith tells of being held captive by bandits, and of fighting 'an awful midnight battle to the very point of surrender with a deadly pack of hungry, wild dogs'. Sporting flowing Arab costume, Frith arrived at Akaba by camel seventy years before Lawrence, where he encountered 'desert princes and rival sheikhs, blazing with jewel-hilted swords'.

During these extraordinary adventures he was assiduously exploring the desert regions bordering the Nile and patiently recording the antiquities and peoples with his camera. He was the first photographer to venture beyond the sixth cataract. Africa was still the mysterious 'Dark Continent', and Stanley and Livingstone's historic meeting was a decade into the future. The conditions for picture taking confound belief. He laboured for hours in his wicker dark-room in the sweltering heat of the desert, while the volatile chemicals fizzed dangerously in their trays. Often he was forced to work in remote tombs and caves where conditions were cooler. Back in London he exhibited his photographs and was 'rapturously cheered' by members of the Royal Society. His reputation as a photographer was made overnight. An eminent modern historian has likened their impact on the population of the time to that on our own generation of the first photographs taken on the surface of the moon.

VENTURE OF A LIFE-TIME

Characteristically, Frith quickly spotted the opportunity to create a new business as a specialist publisher of photographs. He lived in an era of immense and sometimes violent change. For the poor in the early part of Victoria's reign work was a drudge and the hours long, and people had precious little free time to enjoy themselves.

Most had no transport other than a cart or gig at their disposal, and had not travelled far beyond the boundaries of their own town or village. However, by the 1870s, the railways had threaded their way across the country, and Bank Holidays and half-day Saturdays had been made obligatory by Act of Parliament. All of a sudden the ordinary working man and his family were able to enjoy days out and see a little more of the world.

With characteristic business acumen, Francis Frith foresaw that these new tourists would enjoy having souvenirs to commemorate their days out. In 1860 he married Mary Ann Rosling and set out with the intention of photographing every city, town and village in Britain. For the next thirty years he travelled the country by train and by pony and trap, producing fine photographs of seaside resorts and beauty spots that were keenly bought by millions of Victorians. These prints were painstakingly pasted into family albums and pored over during the dark nights of winter, rekindling precious memories of summer excursions.

THE RISE OF FRITH & CO

Frith's studio was soon supplying retail shops all over the country. To meet the demand he gathered about him a small team of photographers, and published the work of independent artist-photographers of the calibre of Roger Fenton and Francis Bedford. In order to gain some understanding of the scale of Frith's business one only has to look at the catalogue issued by Frith & Co in 1886: it runs to some 670

court card, but there was little room for illustration. In 1899, a year after Frith's death, a new card measuring 5.5 x 3.5 inches became the standard format, but it was not until 1902 that the divided back came into being, with address and message on one face and a full-size illustration on the other. *Frith & Co* were in the vanguard of postcard development, and Frith's sons Eustace and Cyril continued their father's monumental task, expanding the number of views offered to the public and recording more and more places in Britain, as the coasts and countryside were opened up to mass travel.

Francis Frith died in 1898 at his villa in Cannes, his great project still growing. The archive he created continued in business for another seventy years. By 1970 it contained over a third of a million pictures of 7,000 cities, towns and villages. The massive photographic record Frith has left to us stands as a living monument to a special and very remarkable man.

pages, listing not only many thousands of views of the British Isles but also many photographs of most European countries, and China, Japan, the USA and Canada – note the sample page shown above from the hand-written *Frith & Co* ledgers detailing pictures taken. By 1890 Frith had created the greatest specialist photographic publishing company in the world, with over 2,000 outlets – more than the combined number that Boots and WH Smith have today! The picture on the right shows the *Frith & Co* display board at Ingleton in the Yorkshire Dales. Beautifully constructed with mahogany frame and gilt inserts, it could display up to a dozen local scenes.

POSTCARD BONANZA

The ever-popular holiday postcard we know today took many years to develop. In 1870 the Post Office issued the first plain cards, with a pre-printed stamp on one face. In 1894 they allowed other publishers' cards to be sent through the mail with an attached adhesive halfpenny stamp. Demand grew rapidly, and in 1895 a new size of postcard was permitted called the

Frith's Archive: *A Unique Legacy*

FRANCIS FRITH'S legacy to us today is of immense significance and value, for the magnificent archive of evocative photographs he created provides a unique record of change in 7,000 cities, towns and villages throughout Britain over a century and more. Frith and his fellow studio photographers revisited locations many times down the years to update their views, compiling for us an enthralling and colourful pageant of British life and character.

We tend to think of Frith's sepia views of Britain as nostalgic, for most of us use them to conjure up memories of places in our own lives with which we have family associations. It often makes us forget that to Francis Frith they were records of daily life as it was actually being lived in the cities, towns and villages of his day. The Victorian age was one of great and often bewildering change for ordinary people, and though the pictures evoke an impression of slower times, life was as busy and hectic as it is today.

We are fortunate that Frith was a photographer of the people, dedicated to recording the minutiae of everyday life. For it is this sheer wealth of visual data, the painstaking chronicle of changes in dress, transport, street layouts, buildings, housing, engineering and landscape that captivates us so much today. His remarkable images offer us a powerful link with the past and with the lives of our ancestors.

TODAY'S TECHNOLOGY

Computers have now made it possible for Frith's many thousands of images to be accessed almost instantly. In the Frith archive today, each photograph is carefully 'digitised' then stored on a CD Rom. Frith archivists can locate a single photograph amongst thousands within seconds. Views can be catalogued and sorted under a variety of categories of place and content to the immediate benefit of researchers. Inexpensive reference prints can be created for them at the touch of a mouse button, and a wide range of books and other printed materials assembled and published for a wider, more general readership - in the next twelve months over a hundred Frith local history titles will be published! The

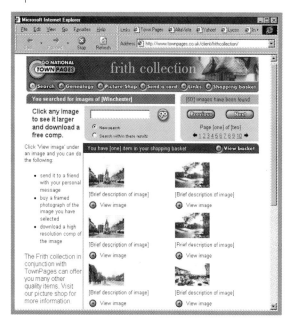

See Frith at www. frithbook.co.uk

day-to-day workings of the archive are very different from how they were in Francis Frith's time: imagine the herculean task of sorting through eleven tons of glass negatives as Frith had to do to locate a particular sequence of pictures! Yet the archive still prides itself on maintaining the same high standards of excellence laid down by Francis Frith, including the painstaking cataloguing and indexing of every view.

It is curious to reflect on how the internet now allows researchers in America and elsewhere greater instant access to the archive than Frith himself ever enjoyed. Many thousands of individual views can be called up on screen within seconds on one of the Frith internet sites, enabling people living continents away to revisit the streets of their ancestral home town, or view places in Britain where they have enjoyed holidays. Many overseas researchers welcome the chance to view special theme selections, such as transport, sports, costume and ancient monuments.

We are certain that Francis Frith would have heartily approved of these modern developments, for he himself was always working at the very limits of Victorian photographic technology.

THE VALUE OF THE ARCHIVE TODAY

Because of the benefits brought by the computer, Frith's images are increasingly studied by social historians, by researchers into genealogy and ancestory, by architects, town planners, and by teachers and schoolchildren involved in local history projects. In addition, the archive offers every one of us a unique opportunity to examine the places where we and our families have lived and worked down the years. Immensely successful in Frith's own era, the archive is now, a century and more on, entering a new phase of popularity.

THE PAST IN TUNE WITH THE FUTURE

Historians consider the Francis Frith Collection to be of prime national importance. It is the only archive of its kind remaining in private ownership and has been valued at a million pounds. However, this figure is now rapidly increasing as digital technology enables more and more people around the world to enjoy its benefits.

Francis Frith's archive is now housed in an historic timber barn in the beautiful village of Teffont in Wiltshire. Its founder would not recognize the archive office as it is today. In place of the many thousands of dusty boxes containing glass plate negatives and an all-pervading odour of photographic chemicals, there are now ranks of computer screens. He would be amazed to watch his images travelling round the world at unimaginable speeds through network and internet lines.

The archive's future is both bright and exciting. Francis Frith, with his unshakeable belief in making photographs available to the greatest number of people, would undoubtedly approve of what is being done today with his lifetime's work. His photographs, depicting our shared past, are now bringing pleasure and enlightenment to millions around the world a century and more after his death.

HERTFORDSHIRE – *An Introduction*

'Hearty, homely, loving Hertfordshire..'
Charles Lamb

ALTHOUGH HERTFORDSHIRE WAS originally one of the six smallest counties in England and Wales, few others, even amongst its counterparts in the Home Counties surrounding London, have been so radically affected by the immense changes wrought by the developments of the past century.

Up until the 17th century Hertfordshire was primarily renowned as an agricultural county, but a deep depression in those markets in 1871, and the increasingly malign influence of London, has meant that today the bulk of its prosperity rests with modern electronic industries and light engineering rather than in the fruits of its soil.

Within its borders, and its straightforward topography, the county incorporates a remarkable variety of landscape, albeit often on an intimate scale. To the north, the extension of the great glacial plain covering Cambridgeshire and Bedfordshire offers vistas of rolling downland, taken up by vast modern prairies of cereal crops. Farther east, where the Rivers Lea, Mimram and Stort wind through their courses, the ancient coppices and woodlands have been retained; the boulder clay topsoil encouraged the planting of barley, making this area the centre of the English malting industry. To the west lie the natural oak and beech woodlands of the Chilterns, while the southern sector of the county still boasts areas of cattle and sheep pastures amid the increasing swathe of new housing estates and industrial expansion.

Even so, more than sixty per cent of its 630 square miles is still taken up by farmland and woods, although the growing pressures and the rapid pace of modern development are inevitably making their presence felt. And certainly no one, including Francis Frith and his associates, could have foreseen how extensively the landscape, along with the small towns and villages of the county, would have altered during the past hundred years.

During the 16th and 17th centuries, many state officials and wealthy merchants had elected to reside in Hertfordshire, and members of other professions, including bankers, duly followed them. They largely invested their riches in improving and enlarging their properties, and in adopting new farming techniques, as well as establishing a number of turnpike trusts to make the roads better. In the Midland Railway extension to London via Bedford, which enabled St. Albans and Harpenden to join the steam age in 1868; finally, the Metropolitan Railway extended to Rickmansworth in 1887 and Chorleywood in 1889. Where the railways went, housing developments quickly followed. The activities of the housebuilding arm of the Metropolitan Railway in particular, whose advertisements promoted the presumed advantages of rural living combined with easy access to London and encouraged the use of the term Metroland, helped to bring about the urbani-

'The garden of England for delight'
Thomas Fuller

turn, these entrepreneurs were followed by other businessmen, and by their clerks, and in due course by an army of wage earners.

Initially, it was the 18th-century navigational improvement of the Rivers Lea and Stort, and the building of the Grand Junction Canal, which made a substantial impact and brought the industrial revolution and the beginnings of a new social order to the county. But these innovations were followed by the advent of the railways, which during the closing decades of the 19th century were to transform the county by allowing people to live in Hertfordshire and commute daily into London. The first main line to open was the London to Birmingham Railway from Euston, which reached Tring in 1837 through Watford and Berkhamstead. The Northern and Eastern railway from Liverpool Street reached Broxbourne and Bishop's Stortford in 1842, and then moved on to Hatfield and Hitchin in 1850. The last of the main lines was sation of vast tracts of former farmland in the south and west. But even as late as 1918, the vast conurbation of London was still largely contained within a six-mile radius of Charing Cross.

Possibly even more important in this process of urban development in the county was the rapid expansion of vehicular transport. Hertfordshire's geographical position to the north of London had prompted the Romans to construct Watling Street, Ermine Street and Akeman Street during the 1st century AD as part of series of radial roads extending out to other parts of England. These roads, along with the ancient east-west Icknield Way, which stretched 190 miles from Hunstanton on the Wash to the vicinity of Stonehenge in Wiltshire, were to provide the basis for the later development of a network of coaching roads and turnpikes. These major routes helped to bring prosperity to the county by fostering trade and encouraging the growth of the small towns along their path. Coaches brought many more travellers onto the roads, and Hertfordshire's place within a day's journey of the capital brought about the establishment of numerous inns during the 18th and 19th centuries when this mode of travel reached its peak.

During the last century, the astonishing growth of motor transport has brought about even more radical changes. Britain's first six-lane motorway, the M1, which was opened in 1959, now cuts through the county from Bushey to Harpenden, while the vastly modified and expanded Great North Road, the A1M, extends from Barnet to Stotfold, and the similarly widened A10 runs along the eastern flank from Waltham Cross up to Royston. The massive road-building programme in the closing decades of this century has also seen the creation of the London orbital M25 motorway, which curves through the southernmost reaches of Hertfordshire and which has, in turn, promoted further extensive building development in the region and an increase in car-travelling commuters.

But quite apart from the effects of modern transport, other factors have helped to swell the county's population from a mere 165,000 people in 1851 to its present level of more than a million. Among the most momentous changes have been those brought about by the foundation of the new Garden Cities: Letchworth in 1903, and Welwyn in the immediate aftermath of the First World War. In addition, following the Second World War, the Labour government implemented some of the recommendations of the wartime County of London plan and designated Stevenage, Hemel Hempstead and Hatfield as new towns. And, as the new millennium dawns, local planning authorities across Hertfordshire are facing up to the challenge of fulfilling new government requirements for housing across the whole of southern England in order to meet the anticipated demands of the 21st century.

Many of the scenes depicted in these pages are no longer recognisable to contemporary residents and visitors to Hertfordshire as a result of the enormous changes that have taken place during the last hundred years. But even amongst the modern constructions of roads, shops, offices and houses which have been created in the small towns and villages during that period, there are still surviving structures which point back to the less frenetic and more tranquil (if demanding) way of life enjoyed by our predecessors. And even if the depredations caused by the demands of an expanding population and modern transport systems have changed the face of Hertfordshire in such a brief period of time, the survival of so much of its countryside bodes well for the future.

'Hertfordshire is England meditative'
E.M.Forster

RICKMANSWORTH, MOOR PARK 1897 39686
The grand frontage of Sir James Thornhill's 18th-century mansion, built in Portland stone and with its gigantic Corinthian portico, situated on a hill overlooking spacious parkland. By the time this picture was taken, the arrival of the Metropolitan railway in the town ten years earlier had seen part of the extensive grounds sold for housing development. The house was no longer lived in after 1921, but serves as a clubhouse for the adjoining golf course and tennis courts.

RICKMANSWORTH, CROXLEY GREEN 1897 39688
A magnificent oak tree dominates the common land and the pleasant nearby houses of this little hamlet on the southern outskirts of Rickmansworth, where, on land to the south-west, the famous Croxley Paper Mills were established on the banks of the river Gade.

RICKMANSWORTH, CHURCH STREET 1897 39675
The square flint tower of St. Mary's church, with its 'Gothic' spike,
dating from 1630, even today still looks down on a thoroughfare
which has retained its country character. Messrs Beeson & Sons, on
the corner of Talbot Road, with its splendid lantern suspended over
the pavement, stocks a complete range of household furnishings,
some of which are displayed not only in the shop windows, but also
in its doorway and along the pavement.

RICKMANSWORTH, HIGH STREET 1897 39673

The next three views give us a novel opportunity to stroll along the High Street over a period of sixty-eight years, and witness some of the numerous changes which took place before its eventual transformation into its present role as a pedestrian precinct. In this photograph the High Street has an almost deserted aspect, apart from two stationary carts; the Post Office is on the left and the Swan Hotel further along on the right.

RICKMANSWORTH
High Street 1921 70498

Now we are a few yards further along the thoroughfare. The
signboard for the Swan Hotel (demolished in 1966) now boasts
a pictorial representation of the bird (even though the
distinctive lantern has been removed) and a new Post Office
building has been opened next door. The shops on the near
left, housing Browns, Percy's the confectioners and Rennie's
opticians, are in a new building, but three doors along the bay-
fronted upper storeys visible in the earlier photograph are still
there. Although the horse-drawn trap shows that motor traffic
has yet to dominate, there are intimations of what lies ahead in
the vehicles parked further on.

RICKMANSWORTH, HIGH STREET c1965 R33065

We have moved nearer still to the bow-fronted building where the street narrows. The motor car has clearly ousted not only the horse but also, apparently, the bicycle. New shop-fronts adorn the premises occupied by Phillips Shoes Limited, DER Television, and the estate agents Locke & Vince on the right, but further along some of the original shop premises survive.

RICKMANSWORTH, THE CANAL AND BATCHWORTH LOCK 1897 39696

This is part of the marvellous system which comprised the Grand Junction or Union Canal, linking the Thames with the Midland canal system, and providing a direct waterway link between London and Birmingham. Completed at the start of the 19th century, it brought the industrial revolution to rural Hertfordshire. Four male generations of one family worked as lock keepers here, providing nearly two hundred years of service between them.

RICKMANSWORTH, THE CANAL 1921 70506
An excellent example of co-operation between bargees on the busy canal network. The two central barges have been lashed together in order to bypass those moored alongside the canal bank. One horse is being led forward along the towpath, and will soon be harnessed up again, while the other waits patiently alongside the adjoining mill. One of the bargees has summoned his wife or daughter to take the tiller, while he stands on the bow ready to cast the towing line ashore.

RICKMANSWORTH, THE OLD MANOR HOUSE 1897 39680
This graceful manor house, built of brick and with a moat, was originally constructed around 1430 near Moor Farm. Cardinal Wolsey substantially enlarged it in 1520, while he was Lord Chancellor.

WATFORD, THE CATHOLIC CHURCH 1906 53622

Dominating its rather mundane surroundings, Holy Rood Church, built between 1883-90, was the inspiration of J F Bentley, later to be the architect of London's Westminster Cathedral, and its brickwork makes exuberant use of traditional Hertfordshire chequerboard effects; he again employed this device in his subsequent masterwork.

WATFORD, CASSIOBURY PARK GATES 1921 70491

From the 17th century through until 1922, Cassiobury Park was the home of the Earls of Essex. The ivy-clad lodge gates, built in 1802, outlasted Cassiobury house itself and were only finally demolished in 1970.

WATFORD
Cassiobury Park and the Canal Lock 1921 70492
Under the magnificent spreading canopy of the Cassiobury
Park trees, just beyond the keeper's cottage, the barge horse
and his female driver enjoy a brief rest while waiting for the
Iron Bridge lock to fill so that the gaily painted butty boats
'Linnett' and 'Evelyn' can continue on their tandem journey
along the Grand Junction Canal, which was redesignated the
Grand Union Canal eight years after this photograph was taken
when it was linked up with seven other canals. Meanwhile, the
bargee waits for the water levels to equalise before he swings the
heavy gates open.

WATFORD, HIGH STREET 1921 70489

On the left is the now sadly demolished Parade, a splendid Gothic construction which, with its intricately patterned brickwork, housed a number of prominent businesses and shops. Just beyond the banner advertising the attractions of the new Shopping Centre was the local branch of J Sainsbury's, with its tiled walls and marble counters, suffused with the subtle and distinctive aromas of cheese and cooked meats.

WATFORD
High Street c1965 W40049
The spacious northern end of the High Street, with its central
water garden and carefully tended flowerbeds, marks the area
where the market hall stood until 1853. The modern shopping
area is dominated by the offices of Eastern Electricity on what
was clearly a very warm summer's day, judging by the number of
opened windows. Very few of the male pedestrians, however, are
prepared to divest themselves of their heavy jackets, and while
the ladies appear more comfortable in their summer dresses,
these full-skirted garments required the under support of
crisply starched petticoats for their effect.

GARSTON, THE MANOR HOUSE c1955 G307002

This early 19th-century listed building, built on the site of the former manor house, has had numerous private owners, reputedly including one eccentric lady with a love of snakes who allowed them to entwine themselves about her person while entertaining guests in the drawing room. In the early stages of the Great War, it was used for billeting soldiers of the London Scottish regiment; but at the time this picture was taken, it was being used by the local hospital group as a Rehabilitation Centre. In 1951 the house and grounds were valued at £21,661, but by 1987 this figure had soared to £1.5 million.

BUSHEY HEATH, ROSARY PRIORY c1955 B415008

Originally Caldecote Towers, this startling edifice was a mid-Victorian private house, built for Captain Marjoribanks Loftus Otway. Described by Pevsner as 'a crazy display.... like a Harrogate hotel', it became Caldicote Towers School in 1891, and then Rosary Priory in 1926, after being acquired by the Dominican Congregation of St Catherine of Suric. It was sold in 1985, and is now Immanuel College, a Jewish secondary school.

BUSHEY, THE POND AND CORONATION ARCH 1953 B414012

Between the Conservative Club building and the stuccoed, wisteria-clad cottages at the Falconer Road end of the High Street, rises the Coronation Arch marking the accession of Queen Elizabeth II to the throne. It followed in the tradition of two earlier arches, also designed by the eighty-year-old local artist Lucy Kemp-Welch, for the 1937 Silver Jubilee of George V and the Coronation of George VI in 1937. This arch was floodlit at night, and stood from June until October, when the materials were then re-utilised in the building of a Scout hut in nearby Little Bushey Lane.

BUSHEY, THE ROYAL MASONIC SENIOR BOYS SCHOOL c1955 B414017

Founded in 1798, with the aim of providing an education to the children of members of the Masonic Order, the school moved to its new buildings at Bushey in 1902. Its design incorporates an odd mixture of styles ranging from Tudor to Gothic, and these were augmented with the further building of science and arts and craft blocks in 1967. The school closed in 1977.

BOREHAMWOOD, GATESHEAD ROAD c1965   B408047

This is an excellent example of the seemingly inexorable tide of uniform London County Council housing which swept northwards to engulf this former hamlet of Elstree after the Second World War. Just over fifty years earlier, the pioneers of the British film industry had based themselves here because of the better lighting conditions away from London's smoke.

BOREHAMWOOD, THEOBALD STREET c1955   B408003

A surviving glimpse of rural Borehamwood before the rash of new building swamped these remnants of village life. Next to the car park of the Crown public house on the right, the creeper-covered cottage advertises the services of the local coal and coke merchant J W Roberts. Ascending the hill into the distance are some of the descendants of the trees of ancient Baram Wood.

BARNET, STREET SCENE C1900 B708001
Although absorbed from Hertfordshire into Greater London in 1965,
Barnet at the turn of the century was a bustling village on the Great North
Road leading out of the rapidly growing metropolis. Standing proudly on
top of the hill on an unsurfaced and heavily trafficked road is the parish
church of St John the Baptist, at the junction of High Street and Wood
Street. Its patterned brickwork and spire were later additions to John
Beauchamp's 15th-century building. On the right is the Bazaar Printing
Office, with a hairdresser's shop on the ground floor.

BARNET, HIGH STREET 1940 B708016

A view down the hill towards London, with the Wellington pub on the right sporting its sign depicting the Duke. By mid-summer the signpost on the lamp standard would have been removed under new war-time emergency regulations and, in the face of increasing food rationing, the branch of United Dairies on the left has elected to spruce up its premises with a new coat of white paint; a useful aid to pedestrians in the stringent blackout conditions. The heavy curtains in the windows above are a further indication of these.

BARNET, STREET SCENE c1965 B708042

A considerable transformation from the scene at the turn of the century, with the macadamised road surface, traffic lights and road islands now channelling the cars and lorries. From the Crown and Anchor pub on the left, the A6 trunk road heads away to Hadley Wood and on to Coventry, while on the right, the gleaming frontage of Clark's shoe shop reflects the passing scene.

TRING
The Park 1897 39651
This imposing 17th-century mansion was originally designed by
Sir Christopher Wren for Henry Guy, and was formerly a home
of the Gore family, before being purchased by the Rothschild
banking family in 1873. The upper storey was added in 1890,
and the old walls encased with red brick and pediments in
1915. The second Lord Rothschild was an enthusiastic, if
eccentric, collector of birds and animals and established the
nearby Zoological Museum in Akeman Street, which he
bequeathed to the British Museum in 1938.

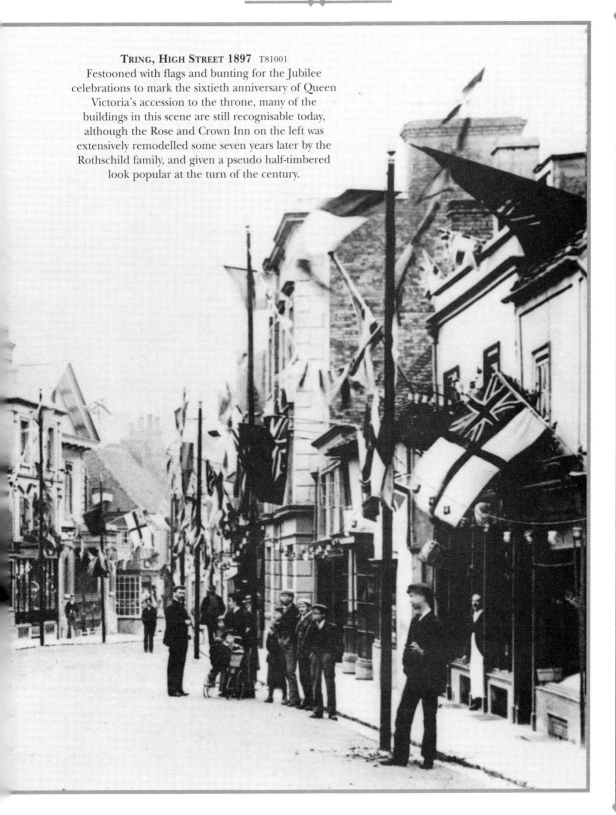

TRING, HIGH STREET 1897 T81001
Festooned with flags and bunting for the Jubilee celebrations to mark the sixtieth anniversary of Queen Victoria's accession to the throne, many of the buildings in this scene are still recognisable today, although the Rose and Crown Inn on the left was extensively remodelled some seven years later by the Rothschild family, and given a pseudo half-timbered look popular at the turn of the century.

NEW MILL, THE CANAL c1955 N153002

NEW MILL
The Canal c1955
A tranquil mid-summer view of the Grand Junction or Union Canal, which reached the nearby town of Tring in 1799 as part of a massive construction, designed to link London and Birmingham and which subsequently had a major impact on the prosperity of the district. A silk factory, established here in 1824, employed several hundred people.

NEW MILL
The Implement Gate c1955
Here we see an imaginative and creative new use for a selection of discarded farm implements, including a scythe, sickles, hay rake, spades, ploughshare and pitchforks, which has become a minor curiosity of this little village on the outskirts of Tring.

NEW MILL, THE IMPLEMENT GATE c1955 N153001

BERKHAMSTED, THE CASTLE C1955 B407050

The dominating centrepiece of the early Norman settlement, the castle with its three moats was built by Robert, Count of Mortain, the half-brother of William the Conqueror. All that now remains of the huge structure, apart from the surrounding earthworks, are the broken ruins of the 12th-century flint and mortar curtain walls within the bailey, which encompass a bowling green and clubhouse. Last occupied in 1496, it was the residence of the Black Prince, and a prison for King John II of France after the Battle of Poitiers in the mid-14th century.

BERKHAMSTED, LOWER KINGS ROAD C1955 B407006

A bustling shopping scene of the early fifties, taken when the row of shops was fairly new. Many of these now await new lessees, but the surmounting clock and its cupola are still present. The greengrocer's shop is still trading, although under another name, but the most surprising aspect to modern eyes will be the evident lack of parking restrictions as evidenced by the line of parked vehicles at the kerbside.

BERKHAMSTED

High Street c1955 B407013

The parish church of St Peter, with its solid flintstone tower
dominating the high street shops and mid-morning traffic in
this picture, was originally built by the Normans alongside the
spacious Roman road. Partly hidden from view, on this side of
the road and by the dry-cleaner's, is the restored Dean Incent's
house with its timbered frontage and leaded glass windows; the
closely neighbouring hostelries of the 17th-century Swan Hotel,
the Crown Inn and the 18th-century King's Arms provide
welcome refreshment and solace for the weary traveller.

BERKHAMSTED
High Street c1955 B407035

A beautifully proportioned view of the High Street, looking
southwards towards St. Peter's Church, whose solid tower is
visible peeking out from behind the building bearing a painted
advertisement for the now defunct Home & Colonial store.
Behind the parked van on the left are the premises once
occupied by W Good's drapery and millinery shop, next to the
ornate facade of the mid-Victorian Town Hall with its clock. Just
beyond that is the White Hart Commercial Hotel. A fancy lamp
standard and horse trough, which were both here in the
twenties, have been replaced by the bus stop and lofty modern
street lamp. The trees on either side of the street are also a
more recent addition of the fifties.

HEMEL HEMPSTEAD
The Marlowes c1965 H255046

The central thoroughfare of the New Town of Hemel
Hempstead, in the prosperous mid-sixties when we'd reputedly
'never had it so good'. The building of the new town centre had
been designated a priority in 1951, and the market moved here
in 1955. The first major chain store to occupy premises in the
new shopping centre, Woolworth's, was quickly followed in 1956
by the Co-operative Stores and Sainsbury's, and in the following
year by Timothy Whites, Boots Chemists and W H Smiths. This
mid-summer picture was obviously taken on a warm day, judging
by the pedestrians in light clothing and the number of open
windows in the offices above Dorothy Perkins
and Burton's tailor shop.

HEMEL HEMPSTEAD, THE MARLOWES C1965 H255007

Another view of this central shopping area, demonstrating the planners' clear intention to incorporate greenery in the shape of existing trees, and the flower boxes on the central island reservation. The parked vehicles on the near side of the road are taxis awaiting hire at the rank, whilst those opposite, including a motorbike and sidecar, are clearly untroubled by any form of contemporary parking restrictions.

HARPENDEN, THE VILLAGE POND 1897 39732

Sad to relate, this restful scene of the village pond in the High Street with its magnificent trees, thatched cottages and elegant pair of swans fell victim to the sweeping expansionism and development of the 20th century. The pond was drained and grassed over during the twenties as the 'highway-valley' village grew into a 'garden-town'.

ST ALBANS, ST PETER'S STREET 1921 70471

George Smith's Town Hall of 1830, which with its Ionic columns and Tuscan pillars bears a remarkable resemblance to the Corn Exchange at Bishop's Stortford and dominates St Peter's Street and its avenue of lime trees planted in 1881. Chequer Street stretches away to the left.

St Albans, Market Place 1921 70475

A closer view of Market Place, minus its Saturday morning stalls and with only the refreshment stand by the lamp-post facing onto the 17th- and 19th-century shops and offices. Those of the clearly emblazoned General Fire & Accident Life Assurance Corporation are among the latter. In the background, a rare town belfry in the shape of the early 15th-century clock tower rises above the roof of a 16th-century building.

St Albans, The Clock Tower and the Market Cross 1921 70477

A rare surviving example of an English belfry, the Clock Tower, built in 1411, stands at the centre of the city with the narrow mediaeval street of French Row on its left and the wider Market Place on its right. The gilt-lettered Red Lion Hotel proudly proclaims its newly-acquired garage facility, while a few doors along this side of the street, next to the over-hanging storeys, is the restored 15th-century Fleur de Lys inn, reputedly named after King John of France who was imprisoned here after the Battle of Poitiers in 1356.

ST ALBANS, HIGH STREET 1921 70476
This view looks northwest up the High Street, towards
the Red Lion Hotel, and the start of George Street, as
a coachman driving a landau prepares to turn right
towards Verulam Road. Of the four parked vehicles
outside the shops, one appears to be in need of
mechanical attention from its uniformed chauffeur.

ST ALBANS
The Abbey 1921 70455
The imposing west front of the Abbey, following the completion
of its restoration thirty years before. The yellow stone and
pepperpot turrets of this 19th-century creation make an odd
contrast with the solid, red Norman tower over the central
transept, but this picture gives a clear impression of the
inordinate length (550 feet) of the church, and an idea of the
effect this must have made on the innumerable mediaeval
pilgrims who travelled here to worship
at the shrine of Saint Alban.

St Albans, Holywell Hill 1921 70479
This peaceful view looks up Holywell Hill towards the city centre, as it dips towards the river and the curative spring from which it takes its name, with, on the right, one of the fine Georgian houses which are a feature of this broad approach to the city's cathedral.

Ayot St Lawrence, The Village c1955 A99009
The sleepy centre of this village, with its picturesque half-timbered cottages and winding lane, was captured from a point near the ruins of the old 14th-century church, which was partly demolished by Sir Lionel Lyde in the late 18th century because it marred his view from new Ayot House.

AYOT ST LAWRENCE, AYOT HOUSE c1955 A99013
The central part of this fine Georgian building became the home of Sir Lionel Lyde, before the later wing on the right was added, and which at the time this picture was taken housed the Lullingstone Silk Farm, to which one of Rugg's coaches has transported a party of visitors. The farm has since moved, and the building is again a private residence.

AYOT ST LAWRENCE, SHAW'S CORNER c1955 A99004
This photograph shows the back of the late-Victorian rectory which became the home of the writer George Bernard Shaw from 1906 until his death in 1950, at the age of ninety-four. Owned by the National Trust, the building houses a number of literary relics, which these visitors have come to peruse. Photographs taken twenty years earlier show this aspect of the building heavily festooned in creepers, which have clearly been severely pruned.

STEVENAGE, KNEBWORTH HOUSE 1899 44274

Knebworth was the home of the Lytton family since they bought the manor in 1492. This view shows the remarkable eastern facade of this Tudor building, partly refashioned some fifty years earlier by Lord Edward Bulwer Lytton in the then fashionable Regency style.

STEVENAGE, HIGH STREET AND THE GREEN 1899 44259

A picturesque collection of cottages and shops line the spacious main street of this Georgian coaching town, as we look towards the triangular Bowling Green, while the photographer's activities attract a considerable degree of interest from onlookers. Even the grocer in his full-length apron has left his counter and come to the door of his shop to view the proceedings.

STEVENAGE, HIGH STREET **1901** 46508
Viewed from the opposite direction and two years after photograph No 44259, the full
expanse of the dusty High Street is apparent, enabling horse-drawn coaches to turn
easily. The avenue of young lime trees was probably planted to mark the sixtieth
jubilee of Queen Victoria. A little girl takes a rest from playing with her hoop, while
behind the lamp-post a young boy leans on a new safety bicycle.

STEVENAGE, HIGH STREET 1903 49771

In the heyday of Stevenage, at the start of the 19th century, up to twenty stagecoaches a day passed along this stretch of the Great North Road. Here, only a peddler's humble donkey waits to cross from the Bowling Green towards the gable end of the Tudor Alleyn's School.

STEVENAGE, HIGH STREET 1903 49772

The White Lion, on the left, was, along with the Cromwell Hotel, the Two Diamonds, and the Yorkshire Grey, among a series of coaching inns spread along the spacious High Street. Even in 1903, the un-made-up road surface bears mute witness to the substantial amount of horse-drawn traffic it carried daily.

STEVENAGE, HIGH STREET 1903 49773
Another view of the dusty, un-made road surface of the High Street which carried so much traffic at the start of the century, together with the intrusive early telegraph poles which, sentinel-like, dwarf the adjacent buildings and trees.

STEVENAGE, HIGH STREET c1965 S191026

This view gives a clear example of the impact commercial motor traffic had on the Great North Road, prior to the building of the M1 motorway. Along with the substantial numbers of parked cars along the verges, a laden lorry and a coach are advancing down the High Street, representative of the immense numbers of similar heavy vehicles which thundered through this part of the old town by day and night. On the left, another lorry awaits an opportunity to join the stream of traffic.

STEVENAGE, COREY'S MILL 1903 49778

The small rural hamlet of Corey's Mill, now completely absorbed into the New Town of Stevenage, was once dominated by its windmill, which burnt down in 1878. Its prominent inn is visible in both this view and in photograph No 49779.

STEVENAGE, COREY'S MILL 1903 49779
The inn was originally called the Harrow, but changed its name to the White Horse in 1769. It stood at the crossroads of the footpath which led from Verulanium (St Albans) via Wheathampstead to Hitchin, once travelled by the Roman legions, mediaeval pilgrims, and by the fugitive King Charles the First while in disguise.

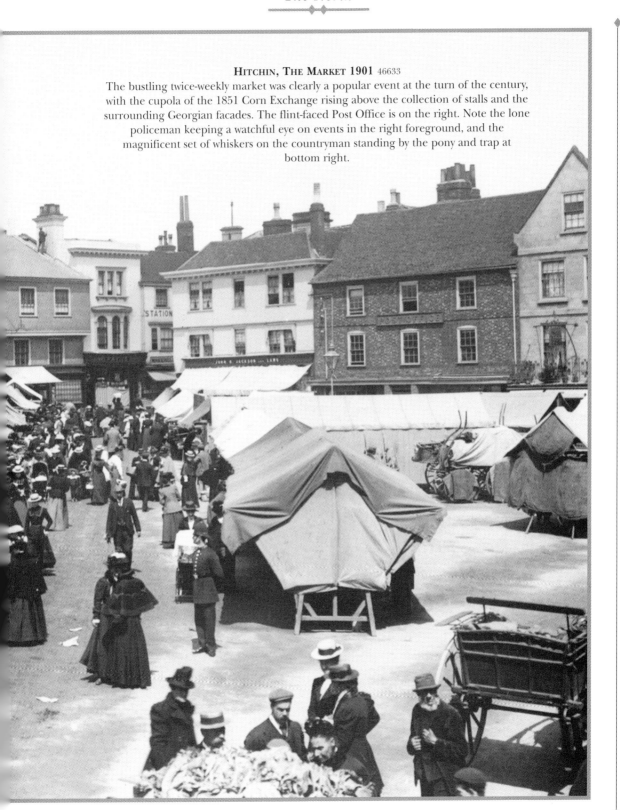

HITCHIN, THE MARKET 1901 46633
The bustling twice-weekly market was clearly a popular event at the turn of the century, with the cupola of the 1851 Corn Exchange rising above the collection of stalls and the surrounding Georgian facades. The flint-faced Post Office is on the right. Note the lone policeman keeping a watchful eye on events in the right foreground, and the magnificent set of whiskers on the countryman standing by the pony and trap at bottom right.

HITCHIN, MARKET PLACE 1922 71893

Already the motor vehicle is making its presence felt in the centre of town. A uniformed chauffeur escorts his employer on her shopping trip, having possibly just left the open-topped car behind. An open-topped double decker bus with its winding stairway takes on passengers, while a covered lorry and other cars are parked on the far side of the market square.

HITCHIN
Market Place c1965 H89027

The internal combustion engine reigns supreme. Viewed from
the opposite angle, the Market Place has been transformed into
a modern car park. The tower and spire of St Mary's Church
rises above the rich assortment of architectural styles, which
range from the 15th to the 20th centuries, with several of the
buildings having recently been given a facelift. Among them are
the drapery firm George Spurr, on the extreme right, and the
rental shop of Bold & Burrows Ltd. The ornately timbered
upper storey of the adjoining shop, formerly Maison Gerard,
now has a modern frontage bearing the name Sarah Lewis.
Already, several of the rooftops boast television aerials.

HITCHIN, HIGH STREET 1903 49736

HITCHIN
High Street 1903

The graceful sweep of the narrow High Street provides the setting for some splendid Victorian shop fronts, with H. Wightman's extended emporium at numbers. 24-5 distinguished by a string of gas lanterns suspended above the pavement. On the right are the adjoining Cock Hotel and Posting House, with the latter having a milestone indicating the distance to London positioned outside the gateway to its stabling area.

◆

HITCHIN
A Backyard 1903

The everyday drudgery of turn of the century life, before modern household appliances eased the burden, is displayed in this portrait of three elderly ladies in this Hitchin backyard. The lady in the centre appears to be the mistress of the house instructing her two servants.

HITCHIN, A BACKYARD 1903 49743

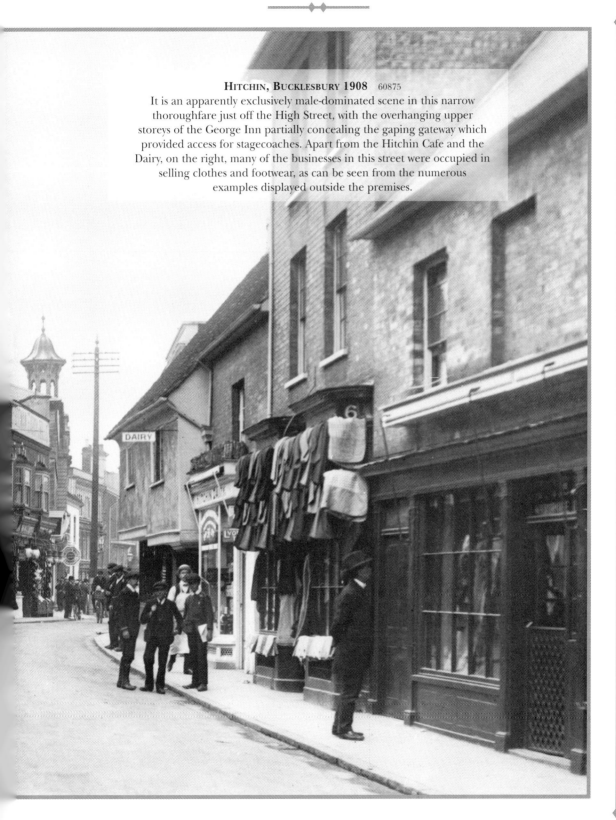

HITCHIN, BUCKLESBURY 1908 60875
It is an apparently exclusively male-dominated scene in this narrow thoroughfare just off the High Street, with the overhanging upper storeys of the George Inn partially concealing the gaping gateway which provided access for stagecoaches. Apart from the Hitchin Cafe and the Dairy, on the right, many of the businesses in this street were occupied in selling clothes and footwear, as can be seen from the numerous examples displayed outside the premises.

HITCHIN, TILEHOUSE STREET 1901 46639

Here we see an architectural paradise. Tilehouse Street, which was named in 1460, incorporates a string of houses dating from the Tudor to the Georgian periods, with many of the earlier buildings refronted with brick and remodelled during the latter era. George Chapman, who translated the works of Homer, was born at No 35 in 1559.

HITCHIN, ST MARY'S CHURCH 1908 60881

The 12th-century tower and spire of St Mary's Church viewed from the Market Place, a symbol of the mediaeval prosperity brought to this little town from wool-trading. Shipley Slipper was a travelling dentist, who visited Hitchin every other Tuesday as part of a practice he established in 1902. Ebenezer Allsop's hosiery and tailoring business was set up at these premises in 1907.

HITCHIN, ST MARY'S CHURCH C1955 H89011

A much busier view of the same scene some forty years after photograph No 60881. The war memorial commemorating the First World War fallen is visible by the church tower, but the adjacent wrought iron gate, railings and lantern have vanished, probably during the scrap metal drive of World War Two. The grocery firm of Halsey & Son were still trading from the same premises, but with a modern shop frontage.

HITCHIN, THE COOPERS ARMS 1903 49745

Cobblestones lead via a spacious entrance into the stableyard of the 16th-century Cooper's Arms in Tilehouse Street with its steeply pitched roof. Its windows incorporated some of the 15th-century tracery from the dismantled Tyler's Guildhall.

HITCHIN, BOYS' GRAMMAR SCHOOL 1901 46643

The school was founded in 1632; its original buildings were supplemented in 1899 by those on the left, at a cost of more than three thousand pounds. They were opened by the then Master of Trinity College Cambridge, the Reverend Butler. They included accommodation for twenty to thirty boarders, as well as a lecture room, large hall and classrooms.

ICKLEFORD, THE CHURCH 1901 46650

Spreading cedar trees frame this southern aspect of St Katherine's Church, with its Early English tower with a weathervane, stuccoed walls and Norman nave. Sir George C Scott carefully restored the building in 1859.

ICKLEFORD, THE VILLAGE 1903 49748

The centre of this straggling village on the outskirts of Hitchin boasted two public houses beside the Green and across the road from the cedars and prominent yew tree in St Katherine's chuchyard. The half-timbered Old George Inn was partly built during the 16th century. On the extreme left is The Green Man, serving Benskin's Ales.

LETCHWORTH, THE CLOISTERS 1908 60889

One of the early buildings constructed as part of Ebenezer Howard's vision of a garden city at Letchworth, this fantastic structure was erected in 1906-7 by the architect Coulishaw, and was intended as a school of theosophical meditation. It made startlingly original use of traditional materials and familiar decoration, but engendered a mixed reaction from critics.

LETCHWORTH, THE HALL HOTEL 1922 71911

This was a feature of the old village of Letchworth, but one which was brought into the master plan for the new garden city. This fine Jacobean mansion with its gables and leaded windows was, as its name indicates, originally an imposing Hall before its transformation into an hotel.

LETCHWORTH, LEY'S AVENUE 1924 75597

Here we see the broad sweep of the garden city's main street looking west, with a wide assortment of businesses lining the wide tree-lined pavements. Most of these shops were built some fifteen years earlier, and the absence of motor vehicles offers a remarkable contrast to the contemporary world.

LETCHWORTH, LEY'S AVENUE 1925 77105

This view shows Ley's Avenue seen from the top of the sloping hill, a year after photograph No 75597, which provides a closer view of the large neo-Georgian-style buildings just visible in the previous photograph.

LETCHWORTH, SPIRELLA CORSET FACTORY 1932 84568

The factory, designed by Cecil Hignett and built between 1912-20, fulfilled Ebenezer Howard's tenet that his Garden City should provide industrial employment and not merely be a dormitory town for London. To William Wallace Kincaid, the American corset manufacturer, Letchworth was the natural choice of site for his first English factory, and it was the city's biggest employer for almost eighty years. With its reinforced concrete and glass structure disguised by brick facings and gabled pavilions, it resembles an updated version of the Arts & Crafts style of architecture.

LETCHWORTH, THE SWIMMING POOL c1950 L39016

The pool is an obvious source of enjoyment and pleasure for the mothers and children of the New Town in this summer scene. The ladies' costumes, though substantially less confining than their pre-war versions, had yet to reach the skimpy fashions of the bikini and the thong of later years.

BALDOCK, WHITE HORSE STREET 1925 77098

Here we see the junction of White Horse Street and Sun Street, leading to St Mary's Church with its 13th-century tower and prominent spike. The oriental turrets of the mid-Victorian red-brick Methodist chapel rising above Wilson's premises on the right are an appropriate reminder that Baldock's name, bestowed by the Knights Templar in the 12th century, means Baghdad.

BALDOCK
White Horse Street 1925 77099
This view looks back towards the site of photograph No 77098.
The Rose & Crown and the Whitehorse Hotel on the right were
among the numerous inns which made this small town one of
Hertfordshire's premier coaching centres, thanks to its position
on the Great North Road and on the important link between
Luton and Royston. The adjacent tobacconist's premises bears
numerous advertisements for assorted products, while on the
opposite side of the street, the hardware store displays some of
its stock, including a roll of wire netting.

BALDOCK, CHURCH STREET 1925 77100
The rear entrance of the White Horse Hotel faces onto Church Street, with a stained glass canopy and hanging baskets above the wide gateway to its garaging and stables. The luxuriant overhanging trees are in the churchyard of St Mary's Church. Two anxious faces (are they the owners of the two parked cars?) peer out of the ground floor window of the hotel.

BALDOCK, HITCHIN STREET 1925 77101
The creeper-clad entrance of the George & Dragon Hotel with its Automobile Association sign shows how rapidly the motor-car was making an impact on society in the years following the First World War.

ASHWELL, THE VILLAGE c1955 A149029
The timbered 16th-century Town House on the left was originally the Abbot of Westminster's Tithe office. Behind its oak timbers infilled with wattle and daub, the local market traders would assemble to pay their dues to their manorial landlord. Later condemned, the cottage was purchased in 1929 for £25 and restored to its original condition to house a small local museum.

ASHWELL, CHANTRY HOUSE c1955 A149028

The thatched Chantry House, on the right, survived the devastating fire of 1795, which destroyed many of the older buildings in this once prosperous mediaeval market town. Concealed from view is its 15th-century traceried window, but the 176-foot tower of the 14th-century church of St Mary's soars as a landmark above the surrounding cottages.

ASHWELL, HIGH STREET c1955 A149007

Here we see some of the other superb buildings dating from the 15th and 17th centuries which escaped three fires in 1632, 1795 and 1850. The close-timbered building on the opposite side of the road is St John's Guildhall, founded in 1476, and partly occupied by Day's bakery. The adjoining building dates from 1681 and features beautiful pargetting on its upper storey.

ROYSTON, GENERAL VIEW 1929 81886

The higgledy-piggledy development of this small country market town which resulted from its unusual position on the county border of Hertfordshire and Cambridgeshire until 1896 is evident in this overall view. Georgian and Victorian red-brick, Tudor timber-frame, and flint-faced buildings are all visible among the trees leading across to the downlands.

ROYSTON, ST BENEDICT'S PRIORY AND MELBOURNE STREET 1929 81896

This patterned red-brick Victorian building was occupied from 1916 onwards by the Benedictine nuns of the Adorers of the Sacred Heart of Jesus, of Montmartre, OSB and used as a novitiate house, before being acquired by the local council, and replaced by the present police station. The building at the crossroads beyond was the Mechanics Institute, built in 1855, and is now the Town Hall. The magnificent horse chestnut trees stand in the Priory Memorial Gardens, where the dead of the First World War are commemorated.

BUNTINGFORD, MARKET HILL 1923 74923

It is towards the end of market day, an event which was revived in 1920. Pens for cattle and sheep can be glimpsed under the trees, and a large lorry waits to carry its four-footed cargo away. The manse, which was the home of the Reverend George Elliot, the congregational minister, was turned into a shop during the nineteen thirties.

BUNTINGFORD, HIGH STREET 1929 81852

This view looks south towards London, along the narrow stretch of Ermine Street or the Old North Road, with its overhanging 17th-century houses and gables. On the left, the line of telegraph poles erected in 1902 hint at modern progress, while on the right the signboard of the George and Dragon surmounts the metal advertising plaques of the surrounding shops.

BUNTINGFORD, HIGH STREET c1955 B245022

We are looking north along the High Street. On the left, between A G Day's, the stationer, newsagent and bookseller's shop and the Angel Inn with its illuminated sign, is the old archway topped by the town clock, all of which are owned by the Buntingford Charity trustees.

BUNTINGFORD, HIGH STREET c1955 B245035

The southern end of the High Street widens slightly here, with houses and an inn just visible behind the line of trees. Across the way, a modern shopfront and sun blind contrast with the picturesque assortment of old cottages and the Black Bull pub stretching away into the distance.

BISHOP'S STORTFORD, MAIN STREET 1899   44880
Unrecognisable today, this peaceful scene is of the present Station Road, with the sign of the old Rose and Crown pub visible in the middle distance on the left. The adjacent cottages have been replaced by the new bus station.

BISHOP'S STORTFORD, WINDHILL 1899 44284
The lofty spire of St Michael's Church is perched above a Perpendicular flint tower topped with a red-brick upper storey. Built in 1812, it rises above this wide street lined with Regency and early Victorian houses and an avenue of lime trees.

BISHOP'S STORTFORD, HOCKERILL STREET 1899 44296
This is the view down Hockerill Street towards the River Stort, where the spire of St Michael's Church rises above the trees and houses. Beyond these charming cottages, at the crossroads at the top end of the hill, were several 16th-century inns, including the Crown, patronised by Daniel Defoe.

BISHOP'S STORTFORD, NORTH STREET 1899 44863

BISHOP'S STORTFORD
North Street 1899

This view was captured from just outside the old Half Moon Hotel, later to become the Urban District Council Offices. Across the way are the printing works of the Herts and Essex Observer newspaper, which also acted as a depot for the publications of the Society for the Propagation of Christian Knowledge. Note the magnificent stag's forequarters mounted over the shopfront further along the street.

◆

BISHOP'S STORTFORD
Windhill 1903

With the tombs and churchyard of St Michael's on the right, the 16th-century Boar's Head Inn and its neighbouring cottages lean over the pavement at the top of Windhill as it drops down towards the High Street.

BISHOP'S STORTFORD, WINDHILL 1903 49754

BISHOP'S STORTFORD, POTTER STREET 1903 49758

Some of the numerous clothing and drapery shops that occupied this part of the town centre can be seen on the left. It had been the scene of a major fire in September 1887 which destroyed what was one of the largest such businesses owned by Robert Lock, who continued to trade for another eight years but went out of business three years before this photograph was taken.

BISHOP'S STORTFORD, NORTH STREET 1903 49757

At the crossroads of Market Place and Potter's Street stands the neo-classical Corn Exchange, designed by Lewis Vulliamy, whose original frontage had a grand entrance dominated by a statue of the harvest goddess Ceres. These were removed and the glass roof substituted to provide adequate light for the grain dealers' rooms. The building also housed the offices of the London and County Bank. The porch on the immediate right is the entrance to the Urban District Council offices.

SAWBRIDGEWORTH, KNIGHT STREET 1903 51095

This view shows a varied mixture of buildings in the central part of this small village, with a tiled dormer-windowed cottage and a weather-boarded two storey house on the left, while on the right stands an attractive red-brick Georgian house between two overhung cottages. An inquisitive dog with a docked tail keeps an attentive eye on proceedings further down the street.

SAWBRIDGEWORTH, THE WHITE LION INN 1903 51097
This junction of two streets marks the site of the former market place, with the stolid red-brick White Lion, on the extreme right, and the King of Prussia pub along the road on the left, ready to slake the thirst of the workers from the maltings and corn mills on which the prosperity of this small town were founded.

SAWBRIDGEWORTH, HYDE HALL 1903 51102
Originally a Tudor house, to the north of the village, the building was remodelled in 1806 by Jeffry Wyatville and given its classical frontage in a manner which was strongly influenced by the work of Sir John Soane.

SAWBRIDGEWORTH, THE RIVER 1903   51104

SAWBRIDGEWORTH
The River 1903
Amid a grove of tall poplars on the banks of the River Stort are the weather-boarded malting mills, which helped to lay the foundation of the town's prosperity following the passing of the Stort Navigation Act of 1768. They were among eighty such enterprises in the county, and much of their product was utilised by the small local breweries, as well as being despatched to London.

◆

HUNSDON
The Turkey Cock c1965
This village watering hole on the road to neighbouring Widford prided itself on being 'the world's most exclusive pub', as evidenced by the signs proclaiming 'No teenager groups served or Teddy Boys' and 'No coaches'. With the decorative wagon wheels, fairy lights, lanterns, horse drawn coaches, and lorry tyres displayed along its frontage, it would be interesting to know what type of clientele its discriminating landlord was seeking.

HUNSDON, THE TURKEY COCK c1965   H475001

HUNSDON, THE GREEN c1965 H475004

The white plastered cottages clustered around the tiny village green and its war memorial date from the 17th century onwards. With its colourful display of carefully tended flowers, spreading chestnut tree and white picket fences, this scene makes for an archetypal illustration of what most people visualise when thinking of an English country village.

STANSTEAD ABBOTS, HIGH STREET 1929 81859

Here we see the lower end of the High Street with the 17th-century Clock House on the opposite side of the T junction, with its mullions, quoins and quaint weather-boarded bell turret. It was formerly used as a school. On the left is the red-brick Pied Bull Inn.

STANSTEAD ABBOTS, HIGH STREET 1929 81862
This is the long, staid High Street of this small village on the banks of the river Lea viewed from the opposite direction from photograph No 81859, with the Pied Bull over on the left, and the bow-fronted houses with their decorative plaques to the immediate right.

STANSTEAD ABBOTS, HIGH STREET 1929 81860
The long, gently sloping High Street is viewed here from its far end, with the partly weather-boarded Rose and Crown coaching inn on the right, and the old Clock House visible in the distance.

STANSTEAD ABBOTS, HIGH STREET C1955 S181021

Apart from the more modern cars parked at the kerbs, little has changed in the village. A bus stop is visible on the right, while an assortment of hardware and ironmongery lines the pavement outside Anderson's store. On the immediate left, the tobacconist and confectioner's shop has some wall-mounted machines dispensing chewing gum and other sweets, as well as a stand advertising Lyons Maid ice cream.

STANSTEAD ST MARGARET'S, THE CROWN INN 1929 81867

The spacious forecourt of the Crown Inn in the neighbouring village of Stanstead St Margaret's, on the opposite bank of the River Lea. The formidable arboreal specimen behind the building may account for the Crown's alternative name of 'The house up a tree'.

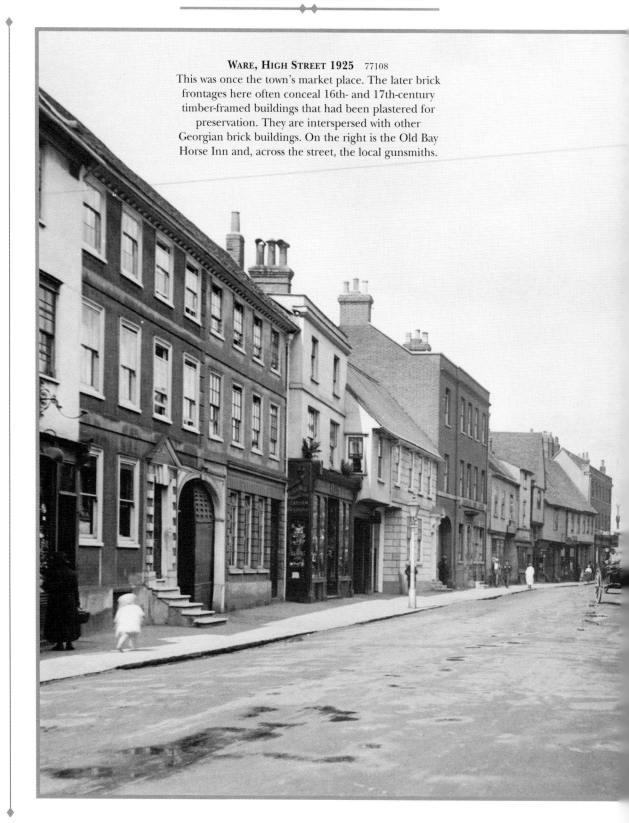

WARE, HIGH STREET 1925 77108
This was once the town's market place. The later brick frontages here often conceal 16th- and 17th-century timber-framed buildings that had been plastered for preservation. They are interspersed with other Georgian brick buildings. On the right is the Old Bay Horse Inn and, across the street, the local gunsmiths.

WARE, HIGH STREET 1925 77109
We are looking north down the High Street towards its division into East and West streets. Motor traffic had yet to make its impact on the town centre, and the forage business run by John Page & Son on the left was still in demand along with its advertised supplies of pet foods.

WARE, HIGH STREET c1955 W24028
Looking north along the High Street, we see that the old lamp standards have been replaced by more lofty modern ones, and while the electrical shop on the left is still primarily concerned with advertising radio appliances from Murphy and Ecko, no doubt television sets are making their presence felt in public demand.

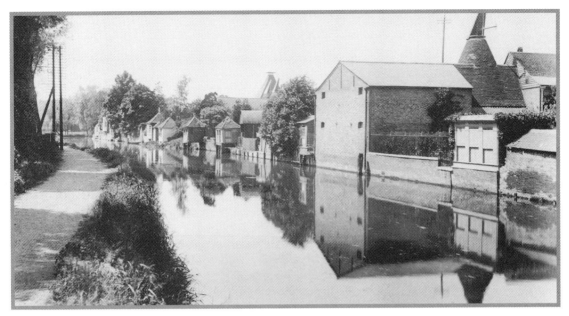

WARE, THE RIVER LEA 1925 77115
The flour and malting mills on the far bank dominate this peaceful riverside scene. From here, the grain barges would travel to London and return with cargoes of coal, helping to make Ware prosperous from the 18th century onwards. Between the mills are a number of ramshackle gazebos belonging to the High Street gardens, projecting out over the calm water and reflected in it.

WARE, FROM SCOTT'S HILL 1929 81838
This peaceful parkland, with trees overhanging the carefully channelled waterway, was the creation of the local 17th-century Quaker poet and writer John Scott, who came to Ware from Bermondsey and used his inheritance to landscape the grounds.

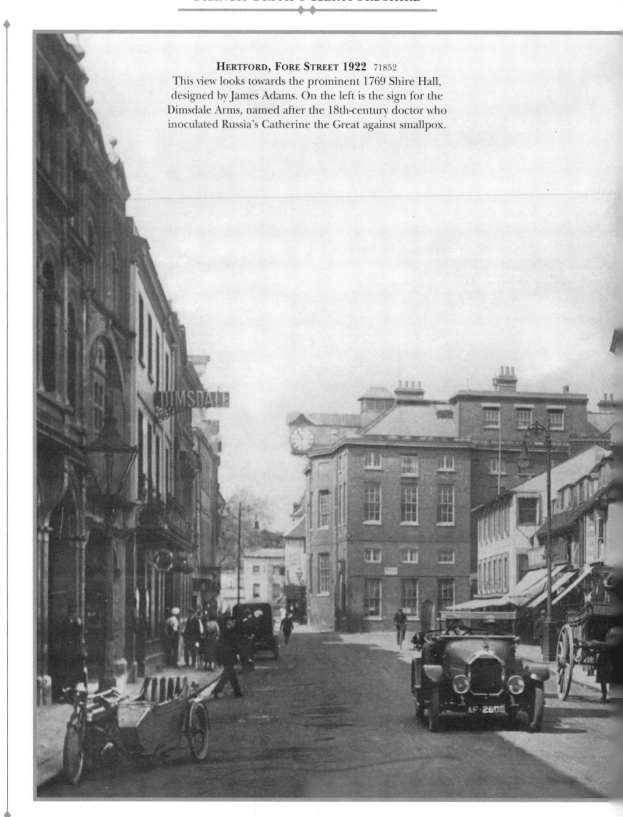

HERTFORD, FORE STREET 1922 71852
This view looks towards the prominent 1769 Shire Hall,
designed by James Adams. On the left is the sign for the
Dimsdale Arms, named after the 18th-century doctor who
inoculated Russia's Catherine the Great against smallpox.

HERTFORD, FORE STREET 1933 85532
The photograph was taken from the centre of the street, showing a banner promoting Hertford's County Hospital, but with many of the same businesses still functioning. Just behind the parked car on the left is the carved entrance to the post office, while on the right a Singer's sign advertises the advantages of sewing on an electrically powered machine.

HERTFORD, FORE STREET 1922 71851
A view from the Shire Hall along what was to become a heavily congested street, until the building of the new relief road, with a string of Georgian and early Victorian shopfronts overshadowed by the 1857 Corn Exchange, likened by Nicolas Pevsner to an 'ambitious Methodist chapel'. An early omnibus collects passengers bound for Ware, Cheshunt, Broxbourne and Waltham Cross from outside Barclays Bank.

HERTFORD, FORE STREET 1933 85533

Little has changed in the intervening eleven years since photograph No 71851 was taken, although more motor vehicles are evident and a double decker bus makes an appearance in the distance. Neale's general store and Dunn's shoe shop are the most prominent emporiums. Within the next decade, the outbreak of the Second World War will necessitate the removal of the statue above the roof of the Corn Exchange to a place of safety.

HERTFORD, MAIDENHEAD STREET 1922 71853

This is one of the major shopping streets of the county town, with the entrance to Pratt's fancy goods store draped with a variety of baskets and bags. On the opposite corner stand the grandiose offices and showroom of the North Metropolitan Electric Company.

HERTFORD, QUEEN'S ROAD 1922 71854
Savagely pollarded lime trees line this quiet residential street with its bijou Victorian villas, several of which on the left have drawn their curtains, or lowered blinds, against the deleterious effects of the early summer sun.

HERTFORD, THE LOCK 1920 81783
John Smeaton and Thomas Telford were among the 18th-century engineers who designed this essential section of the Lea Navigation Canal and River Lea, which allowed hundred-ton ships to reach Hertford and transport cargoes of malt to London. The lock allowed the maintenance of the necessary water levels downstream to Dicker's Mill.

HERTFORD, PORT HILL 1929 81776

Still recognisable today, this steep hill leading towards Bengeo must have posed a challenge to early motor vehicles. The Reindeer Inn on the left was originally a house called The Running Deer in 1740, owned by the Dunster family. The Reindeer was first licensed in 1837, and is still a public house - but renamed The Hodden Horse Too.

HERTFORD, THE WAR MEMORIAL 1933 85536

The war memorial, surmounted by the stag, which is the county symbol, stands at the junction of St Andrews Street and Fore Street. Beyond the cars and omnibuses are the clock on the Shire Hall and the frontage of the Corn Exchange.

WELWYN GARDEN CITY, THE VIADUCT c1955 W294054

Here we see some of the forty arches of the Digswell, or Welwyn viaduct, built between 1848 and 1850 out of bricks fired on the site. Designed by Lewis Cubitt, it rises at its highest point to more than thirty metres above the River Mimram and dominates the surrounding area.

WELWYN GARDEN CITY, STONE HILLS c1960 W294055

Is this how Ebenezer Howard envisioned that his second Utopia would eventually look, when he founded it in 1919? The neo-Georgian shops and offices, designed by chief architect Louis de Soissons, stand on broad boulevards, with spacious pavements, but the ubiquitous car is already beginning to impose its own demands on the local population.

HODDESDON, BURFORD STREET AND THE CLOCK TOWER c1950 H259015
After the First World War, the former Market Place was congregated here around the 1835 brick clock tower, built on the site of a mediaeval chapel. Looking north into the distance, one can see the oncoming, creeping tide of housing development which now links Hoddesdon, Cheshunt and Broxbourne together.

HODDESDON, THE FISH AND EELS HOTEL c1960 H259110
A few minutes from the centre of the original village and situated by the weir, this small 19th-century hotel on the banks of the River Lea, with its eight rooms, was, and still is, popular with anglers and other sportsmen. It has been radically expanded within the last decade with the construction of a much larger extension, and no longer provides accommodation.

HODDESDON, THE SHOPPING PRECINCT c1960 H259115

The brash sixties shopping precinct is overlooked by its nine-storey block of flats (with some evidently still awaiting occupation according to the sign); the tower of St Paul's Church rises among the trees in the background.

HODDESDON, THE SHOPPING PRECINCT c1960 H259118

Here we see another view of the bleak and unappealing shopping precinct, constructed when the town's population numbered less than twenty thousand people; it appears less incongruous when viewed alongside the other more recent developments in the town.

HODDESDON, RYE HOUSE 1904 51417

HODDESDON
Rye House 1904
The front aspect of the mid-15th-century red brick gatehouse of Rye House, the scene of the ill-fated 1683 Whig conspiracy to ambush Charles II as he returned to London from Newmarket, which was foiled when the plotters were betrayed and subsequently executed.

◆

HODDESDON
Rye House 1904
These are the public gardens behind the gatehouse, with its modern glass conservatories and colourful flowerbeds lined with benches. All have been recently restored by the Department of the Environment. The gatehouse, with its red brick and blue diapering, was the earliest major brickwork in the county.

HODDESDON, RYE HOUSE 1904 51418A

BROXBOURNE, THE RIVER C1960 B413031
Here we see the peaceful banks of the New River, with houseboats and leisure craft moored alongside. The arrival of the New River provided the stimulus for the development of Broxbourne in the early 17th century.

BROXBOURNE, VAN HAGE'S NURSERIES C1960 H259094
Established on the derelict site of Spitlebrook Farm in 1953 by the Dutch couple Mr and Mrs Van Hage, these nurseries were among the very first garden centres to be set up in Britain. This water cascade and windmill fronting onto the main road through Broxbourne was a familiar landmark until 1968, when the family business moved to its present location at Great Amwell; this site was developed as a block of modern luxury apartments.

BROXBOURNE, THE STATION c1960 B413067

The coming of the railway to Broxbourne in 1840 had further stimulated the growth of the village, and demand from London-bound commuters heading for Liverpool Street and St. Pancras, and the development of the service, eventually required the building of this new station in 1960. It was praised as one of the first good modern stations. Although the line was electrified as part of the modernisation scheme, steam trains were also still in operation, as can be seen across the far platform.

CHESHUNT, TEMPLE BAR c1960 C319035

Temple Bar was designed by Sir Christopher Wren in 1672, to replace the earlier City of London gate destroyed by the Great Fire, and was the last of the old city gates to survive. But because of the enormous growth in London traffic during the Victorian era, it was dismantled in 1878, and acquired by Sir Henry Meux as the entrance to the family estate at Theobald's Park. In recent years the statues have been removed and the structure boarded up to prevent further dilapidation.

CHESHUNT
St Mary's Parish Church c1960
The 15th-century stone tower of this Perpendicular church situated in the heart of the old village, with its 17th-century cupola on the stair turret, was heavily restored during the 19th century, partly by Bodley.

CHESHUNT
The Roundabout c1960
This is part of modern Cheshunt, with its brash new shopping parade and roundabout with its ornamental fountain, which would not be out of place in one of Hertfordshire's new towns. The advertising hoarding on the left carries posters urging membership of the Labour Party.

CHESHUNT, ST MARY'S PARISH CHURCH c1960 C319045

CHESHUNT, THE ROUNDABOUT c1960 C319039

CHESHUNT, TURNER'S HILL c1960 C319041

This view from the roundabout looks north along Turner's Hill, where the contrast between the modern shopping parade and the smaller old shops can be appreciated. On the far side is the modern brick branch of the Midland Bank, while on the immediate right are the Post Office, chemists and opticians.

CHESHUNT, STREET SCENE c1960 C319046

A line of parked cars, and a frozen foods van making a delivery, marks this mid-summer morning scene along the shopping centre of the village which, at the time, was already rapidly expanding.

WALTHAM CROSS, THE CROSS 1904 51428

The original Eleanor Cross, one of twelve erected by Edward I along the route taken by his wife's funeral cortege, was built in 1291 from Caen stone and Sussex and Purbeck marble and inset with precious stones. It dominated the busy crossroads and provided the name for this small hamlet on the southern outskirts of Cheshunt. The railings were installed during mid-Victorian restoration, and the original statues are now in Cheshunt public library.

WALTHAM CROSS, THE FOURE SWANNES HOTEL 1921 70173

The spacious frontage of the 13th-century hotel, with the Eleanor Cross just visible beyond, was clearly promoting its new services at the start of the motoring age. Today, only the gallows pole across the street remains of its distinctive sign, while the building itself, along with Kemp's the bootmaker's, has been replaced by a massive new shopping centre.

WALTHAM CROSS, HIGH STREET 1921 70172
The ornate Victorian shop fronts of Dawson's and the branch of the Enfield Co-operative store, on the right, with their elegant lanterns, are in contrast to the stern brick frontages across the street.

WALTHAM CROSS, THE POST OFFICE AND HIGH STREET c1950 W163009
This bustling fifties shopping scene, with a substantial and surprising number of bicycles in evidence, shows the prominent red-brick Post Office on the left standing out against its rather dingy neighbouring buildings.

Index

Frith Book Co Titles

Frith Book Company publish over a 100 new titles each year. For latest catalogue please contact Frith Book Co.

Town Books 96pp, 100 photos. County and Themed Books 128pp, 150 photos (unless specified) All titles hardback laminated case and jacket except those indicated pb (paperback)

Around Bakewell	1-85937-113-2	£12.99	Isle of Man	1-85937-065-9	£14.99
Around Barnstaple	1-85937-084-5	£12.99	Isle of Wight	1-85937-114-0	£14.99
Around Bath	1-85937-097-7	£12.99	Around Leicester	1-85937-073-x	£12.99
Around Blackpool	1-85937-049-7	£12.99	Around Lincoln	1-85937-111-6	£12.99
Around Bognor Regis	1-85937-055-1	£12.99	Around Liverpool	1-85937-051-9	£12.99
Around Bournemouth	1-85937-067-5	£12.99	Around Maidstone	1-85937-056-X	£12.99
Around Bristol	1-85937-050-0	£12.99	North Yorkshire	1-85937-048-9	£14.99
British Life A Century Ago	1-85937-103-5	£17.99	Northumberland and Tyne & Wear		
Around Cambridge	1-85937-092-6	£12.99		1-85937-072-1	£14.99
Cambridgeshire	1-85937-086-1	£14.99	Around Nottingham	1-85937-060-8	£12.99
Cheshire	1-85937-045-4	£14.99	Around Oxford	1-85937-096-9	£12.99
Around Chester	1-85937-090-X	£12.99	Oxfordshire	1-85937-076-4	£14.99
Around Chesterfield	1-85937-071-3	£12.99	Around Penzance	1-85937-069-1	£12.99
Around Chichester	1-85937-089-6	£12.99	Around Plymouth	1-85937-119-1	£12.99
Cornwall	1-85937-054-3	£14.99	Around Reading	1-85937-087-X	£12.99
Cotswolds	1-85937-099-3	£14.99	Around St Ives	1-85937-068-3	£12.99
Cumbria	1-85937-101-9	£14.99	Around Salisbury	1-85937-091-8	£12.99
Around Derby	1-85937-046-2	£12.99	Around Scarborough	1-85937-104-3	£12.99
Devon	1-85937-052-7	£14.99	Scottish Castles	1-85937-077-2	£14.99
Dorset	1-85937-075-6	£14.99	Around Sevenoaks and Tonbridge		
Dorset Coast	1-85937-062-4	£14.99		1-85937-057-8	£12.99
Down the Thames	1-85937-121-3	£14.99	Sheffield and S Yorkshire	1-85937-070-5	£14.99
Around Dublin	1-85937-058-6	£12.99	Around Southport	1-85937-106-x	£12.99
East Anglia	1-85937-059-4	£14.99	Around Shrewsbury	1-85937-110-8	£12.99
Around Eastbourne	1-85937-061-6	£12.99	Shropshire	1-85937-083-7	£14.99
English Castles	1-85937-078-0	£14.99	South Devon Coast	1-85937-107-8	£14.99
Essex	1-85937-082-9	£14.99	Staffordshire (96pp)	1-85937-047-0	£12.99
Around Exeter	1-85937-126-4	£12.99	Around Stratford upon Avon		
Around Falmouth	1-85937-066-7	£12.99		1-85937-098-5	£12.99
Around Great Yarmouth	1-85937-085-3	£12.99	Suffolk	1-85937-074-8	£14.99
Greater Manchester	1-85937-108-6	£14.99	Surrey	1-85937-081-0	£14.99
Hampshire	1-85937-064-0	£14.99	Around Torbay	1-85937-063-2	£12.99
Around Harrogate	1-85937-112-4	£12.99	Welsh Castles	1-85937-120-5	£14.99
Hertfordshire	1-85937-079-9	£14.99	West Midlands	1-85937-109-4	£14.99
			Wiltshire	1-85937-053-5	£14.99

Frith Book Co Titles Available in 2000

Canals and Waterways	1-85937-129-9	£17.99	Apr
Around Guildford	1-85937-117-5	£12.99	Apr
Around Horsham	1-85937-127-2	£12.99	Apr
Around Ipswich	1-85937-133-7	£12.99	Apr
Ireland (pb)	1-85937-181-7	£9.99	Apr
London (pb)	1-85937-183-3	£9.99	Apr
New Forest	1-85937-128-0	£14.99	Apr
Around Newark	1-85937-105-1	£12.99	Apr
Around Newquay	1-85937-140-x	£12.99	Apr
Scotland (pb)	1-85937-182-5	£9.99	Apr
Around Southampton	1-85937-088-8	£12.99	Apr
Sussex (pb)	1-85937-184-1	£9.99	Apr
Around Winchester	1-85937-139-6	£12.99	Apr
Around Belfast	1-85937-094-2	£12.99	May
Colchester (pb)	1-85937-188-4	£8.99	May
Dartmoor	1-85937-145-0	£14.99	May
Exmoor	1-85937-132-9	£14.99	May
Leicestershire (pb)	1-85937-185-x	£9.99	May
Lincolnshire	1-85937-135-3	£14.99	May
North Devon Coast	1-85937-146-9	£14.99	May
Nottinghamshire (pb)	1-85937-187-6	£9.99	May
Peak District	1-85937-100-0	£14.99	May
Redhill to Reigate	1-85937-137-x	£12.99	May
Around Truro	1-85937-147-7	£12.99	May
Yorkshire (pb)	1-85937-186-8	£9.99	May
Berkshire (pb)	1-85937-191-4	£9.99	Jun
Brighton (pb)	1-85937-192-2	£8.99	Jun
Churches of Berkshire	1-85937-170-1	£17.99	Jun
Churches of Dorset	1-85937-172-8	£17.99	Jun
Derbyshire (pb)	1-85937-196-5	£9.99	Jun
East Sussex	1-85937-130-2	£14.99	Jun
Edinburgh (pb)	1-85937-193-0	£8.99	Jun
Norwich (pb)	1-85937-194-9	£8.99	Jun
South Devon Living Memories			
	1-85937-168-x	£14.99	Jun

Stone Circles & Ancient Monuments			
	1-85937-143-4	£17.99	Jun
Victorian & Edwardian Kent			
	1-85937-149-3	£14.99	Jun
Warwickshire (pb)	1-85937-203-1	£9.99	Jun
Buckinghamshire (pb)	1-85937-200-7	£9.99	Jul
Down the Severn	1-85937-118-3	£14.99	Jul
Kent (pb)	1-85937-189-2	£9.99	Jul
Victorian & Edwardian Yorkshire			
	1-85937-154-x	£14.99	Jul
West Sussex	1-85937-148-5	£14.99	Jul
Cornish Coast	1-85937-163-9	£14.99	Aug
County Durham	1-85937-123-x	£14.99	Aug
Croydon Living Memories	1-85937-162-0	£12.99	Aug
Dorsert Living Memories	1-85937-210-4	£14.99	Aug
Glasgow (pb)	1-85937-190-6	£8.99	Aug
Gloucestershire	1-85937-102-7	£14.99	Aug
Herefordshire	1-85937-174-4	£14.99	Aug
Kent Living Memories	1-85937-125-6	£14.99	Aug
Lancashire (pb)	1-85937-197-3	£9.99	Aug
Manchester (pb)	1-85937-198-1	£8.99	Aug
North London	1-85937-206-6	£14.99	Aug
Somerset	1-85937-153-1	£14.99	Aug
Tees Valley & Cleveland	1-85937-211-2	£14.99	Aug
Worcestershire	1-85937-152-3	£14.99	Aug
Victorian & Edwardian Maritime Album			
	1-85937-144-2	£17.99	Aug

Available from your local bookshop or from the publisher

FRITH PRODUCTS & SERVICES

Francis Frith would doubtless be pleased to know that the pioneering publishing venture he started in 1860 still continues today. More than a hundred and thirty years later, The Francis Frith Collection continues in the same innovative tradition and is now one of the foremost publishers of vintage photographs in the world. Some of the current activities include:

Interior Decoration

Today Frith's photographs can be seen framed and as giant wall murals in thousands of pubs, restaurants, hotels, banks, retail stores and other public buildings throughout the country. In every case they enhance the unique local atmosphere of the places they depict and provide reminders of gentler days in an increasingly busy and frenetic world.

Product Promotions

Frith products have been used by many major companies to promote the sales of their own products or to reinforce their own history and heritage. Brands include Hovis bread, Courage beers, Scots Porage Oats, Colman's mustard, Cadbury's foods, Mellow Birds coffee, Dunhill pipe tobacco, Guinness, and Bulmer's Cider.

Genealogy and Family History

As the interest in family history and roots grows world-wide, more and more people are turning to Frith's photographs of Great Britain for images of the towns, villages and streets where their ancestors lived; and, of course, photographs of the churches and chapels where their ancestors were christened, married and buried are an essential part of every genealogy tree and family album.

A series of easy-to-use CD Roms is planned for publication, and an increasing number of Frith photographs will be able to be viewed on specialist genealogy sites. A growing range of Frith books will be available on CD.

The Internet

Already thousands of Frith photographs can be viewed and purchased on the internet. By the end of the year 2000 some 60,000 Frith photographs will be available on the internet. The number of sites is constantly expanding, each focussing on different products and services from the Collection.
Some of the sites are listed below.
www.townpages.co.uk
www.icollector.com
www.barclaysquare.co.uk
www.cornwall-online.co.uk

For background information on the Collection look at the two following sites:
www.francisfrith.com
www.francisfrith.co.uk
www.frithbook.co.uk

Frith Products

All Frith photographs are available Framed or just as Mounted Prints, and can be ordered from the address below. From time to time other products - Address Books, Calendars, Table Mats, Postcards etc - are available.

The Frith Collectors' Guild

In response to the many customers who enjoy collecting Frith photographs we have created the Frith Collectors' Guild. Members are entitled to a range of benefits, including a regular magazine, special discounts and special limited edition products.

For further information: if you would like further information on any of the above aspects of the Frith business please contact us at the address below:
The Francis Frith Collection, Frith's Barn, Teffont, Salisbury, Wiltshire England SP3 5QP.
Tel: +44 (0) 1722 716 376 Fax: +44 (0) 1722 716 881 Email: uksales@francisfrith.com

To receive your FREE Mounted Print

Mounted Print
Overall size 14 x 11 inches

Cut out this Voucher and return it with your remittance for £1.50 to cover postage and handling. Choose any photograph included in this book. Your SEPIA print will be A4 in size, and mounted in a cream mount with burgundy rule lines, overall size 14 x 11 inches.

Order additional Mounted Prints at HALF PRICE (only £7.49 each*)

If there are further pictures you would like to order, possibly as gifts for friends and family, acquire them at half price (no additional postage and handling required).

Have your Mounted Prints framed*

For an additional £14.95 per print you can have your chosen Mounted Print framed in an elegant polished wood and gilt moulding, overall size 16 x 13 inches (no additional postage and handling required).

---

* IMPORTANT!
These special prices are only available if ordered using the original voucher on this page (no copies permitted) and at the same time as your free Mounted Print, for delivery to the same address

Frith Collectors' Guild

From time to time we publish a magazine of news and stories about Frith photographs and further special offers of Frith products. If you would like 12 months FREE membership, please return this form.

Send completed forms to:
The Francis Frith Collection, Frith's Barn, Teffont, Salisbury, Wiltshire SP3 5QP

for FREE and Reduced Price Frith Prints

Picture no.	Page number	Qty	Mounted @ £7.49	Framed + £14.95	Total Cost
		1	**Free of charge***	£	£
			£7.49	£	£
			£7.49	£	£
			£7.49	£	£
			£7.49	£	£
			£7.49	£	£

Please allow 28 days for delivery	* Post & handling	£1.50
Book Title	**Total Order Cost**	£

Please do not photocopy this voucher. Only the original is valid, so please cut it out and return it to us.

I enclose a cheque / postal order for £ . . . . made payable to 'The Francis Frith Collection'
OR please debit my Mastercard / Visa / Switch / Amex card

Number . . . .

Expires . . . .   Signature . . . .

Name Mr/Mrs/Ms . . . .

Address . . . .

. . . .

. . . .

. . . . Postcode . . . .

Daytime Tel No . . . .   Valid to 31/12/01

The Francis Frith Collectors' Guild

Please enrol me as a member for 12 months free of charge.

Name Mr/Mrs/Ms . . . .

Address . . . .

. . . .

. . . .

. . . . Postcode . . . .

Free Print - see overleaf